In the tree

Written by Keith Gaines

Illustrated by Margaret de Souza

Nelson

"Look at the cat,"
said Rob.
"The cat is up in the tree.
Get down, cat."

"Get down, cat,"
said Kim.

Kim clapped her hands,
but the cat just sat
in the tree.

"Get down cat,"
said Rob.

Rob stamped his feet,
but the cat just sat
in the tree.

Rob threw his hat at the cat,
but the cat just sat
in the tree.

"I will get the cat down," said Rob.
"Help me get up the tree.

You bend down and
I will get on your back."

"Come here, cat,"
said Rob.
"Come to me."

The cat did not come to Rob.
It just sat in the tree.

"I will get up into the tree," said Rob.
"I will get that cat."

The cat ran down the tree.

The cat jumped onto the car.

The cat ran to Kim.

"The cat is with me,"
said Kim.
"Come down, Rob."

"I can't get down,"
said Rob.
"Help me get down."

"Look at Rob,"
said Kim.
"He is up in the tree.
Get down, Rob."

But Rob just sat in the tree.